S

The Vic

Written by Sally Hewitt

W
FRANKLIN WATTS
LONDON·SYDNEY

First published in 2006 by Franklin Watts
338 Euston Road, London NW1 3BH

Franklin Watts Australia
Hachette Children's Books
Level 17/207 Kent Street, Sydney NSW 2000

Editor: Rachel Tonkin
Designers: Rachel Hamdi and Holly Mann
Picture researcher: Diana Morris
Craft projects: Rachel Tonkin

Picture credits:
Bridgeman Art Library: 20tr; British Library/HIP/Topfoto: 6,
26b; Corbis: 23t; Corporation of London /HIP/Topham: 24t;
Mary Evans Picture Library: front cover, 12t, 15t, 25t, 27t, 27b;
Fotomas/Topham: 13t, 16b, 17t; HIP/Topfoto: 7c; Museum of
London/HIP/Topfoto: 10t; Photri/Topham: 16t;
Picturepoint/Topham: 6b, 8b, 12b, 19; Roger-Viollet/Topham:
24b; Ronald Sheridan/AAAC/Topham: 22; Topfoto: 7b, 9tr, 10b,
14, 18t; Woodmansterne/Topham: 18b.

With thanks to our model: Emel Augustin

A CIP catalogue record for this book
is available from the British Library

ISBN: 978 0 7496 6500 5
Dewey Classification: 941.081

Printed in China

Franklin Watts is a division of Hachette Children's Books.

Contents ■ ■ ■

The Victorians

Queen Victoria's **reign** w
the longest of any Briti
or queen. It lasted fo
and is known as the
Age. During this time
the British **Empire** be
the biggest and mos
powerful empire in the

Queen Victoria,
who reigned from
1837 to 1901.

fam
dro

Industry and technology

The Victorians built factories across the country. **Steam engines** drove machines that wove cotton and made goods. Bridges and giant steam ships were built from iron and steel. Railways ran from city to city.

Workers using the machines at a Victorian blanket factory.

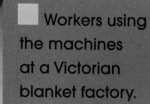 The first telephone call was made during the Victorian Age.

Work and education

During the Victorian Age, working people earned better wages than ever before and **working conditions** improved. All children had the chance to go to school.

Queen Victoria

The young Victoria hardly ever played with other children. She had lessons alone and had to obey very strict rules. She sketched and painted, played the piano, learnt to dance and kept a diary.

When Victoria was 21 she married her cousin Albert.

Victoria and Albert had nine children.

Main events of Victoria's life

1819 – Victoria born in London

1837 – Victoria becomes queen aged 18. She was crowned a year later

1840 – She marries her German cousin, Prince Albert

1861 – Albert dies of **typhoid**

1897 – Queen Victoria celebrates her Golden Jubilee – 50 years on the throne

1901 – Victoria dies aged 81

When Prince Albert died, Queen Victoria didn't appear in public for 13 years. This made her unpopular. The Victorians wanted her to look and act like their queen.

A painting of Victoria in her coronation robes and crown.

Make a collage crown

The crown is a symbol of royalty, wealth and power.

▶ 1 Copy the shape of the crown onto a piece of card about the width of your head.

▶ 3 Stick the material and decorations onto the crown outline. Make it look as sparkling as you can. Add a band of thick card to go around your head.

▶ 2 Collect shiny material, sequins, glitter, cotton wool and plastic jewels to decorate your crown.

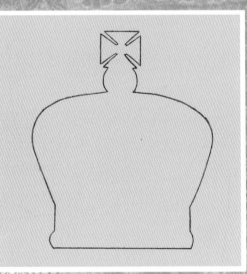

Middle-class homes

Family life was important to the Victorians.
In a **middle-class** home, fathers worked and provided for the family. Mothers stayed at home to look after the children and run the house.

Families entertained themselves in the evenings.

Servants worked hard from morning to night.

Housework

Victorian housework was hard work! Fires had to be lit for heating, cooking and hot water. Floors were scrubbed and washing was done by hand. A middle-class family had servants to cook and clean for them and a nanny to look after the children.

Mrs Beeton's *Book of Household Management* had 1,300 recipes and tips for Victorian housewives. It sold two million copies.

Ingredients

9 slices of bread, cut into triangles • butter for spreading • 110g currants • 900ml milk • sugar, to taste • few drops of vanilla essence • 4 eggs

Cook a Mrs Beeton recipe (adapted)

Baked bread and butter pudding was filling, cheap to make and could be served all year round.

▶ 1 Butter the triangles of bread and place them in a pie dish. Sprinkle currants between each layer and on the top.

▶ 3 Pour the milk mixture over the bread and butter and bake at 160°C (gas mark 3) for 1 hour.

▶ 2 Sweeten the milk with a little sugar and add the vanilla essence. Whisk the eggs and stir into the milk.

Modern tips

• Use thin sliced bread.

• Sprinkle a little sugar on top before you bake it to get a crunchy crust.

• Serve with cream or custard.

Childhood

In a middle-class home, Victorian children spent the day in the **nursery** where they played, had lessons and ate their meals. They walked in the park with their nanny for fresh air and exercise.

The nanny looked after the children and mended their clothes.

Books

Some Victorian children's books, such as *Alice in Wonderland, Treasure Island* and *The Jungle Book*, are still popular today.

Victorian dolls were expensive.

Toys

Toys were looked after with great care. These dolls' faces are made of china. They have real hair and lace clothes.

In the street

Children from poor homes often played hopscotch and tag in the street. They made simple toys such as a wooden hoop.

Poor children often had to make toys from odds and ends.

Cup and ball game

Make the simple Victorian cup and ball game.

▶ 1 Cut 1cm off the bottom of a paper cup. Push a cardboard tube through the hole and overlap by 4cm; tape in position.

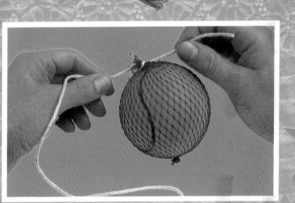

▶ 2 Make a small hole in the cup near the top rim. Attach a piece of string 40cm long.

▶ 3 Push a foam tennis ball into some netting (from a bag of fruit). Tie one end up with the string and secure the other end with thread. See if you can catch the ball in the cup!

School

At the beginning of the Victorian Age, middle-class children were taught at home by a **governess** or tutor. Older boys went to **boarding school**. There were charity schools for the poor, but many children never went to school.

Education for all

In 1870, **Board Schools**, paid for by local taxes, were set up.

Children learnt the three Rs – reading, writing and arithmetic.

They did physical exercise called drill. Boys did woodwork and girls learnt to cook.

By the end of the Victorian Age, all children between the ages of 5 and 13 had to go to school by law.

Children used chalk and a slate to write on.

Sewing

Victorian girls sewed **samplers** to hang on the wall at home. A sampler often included the alphabet, numbers and an uplifting saying or rhyme or a verse from the Bible. It was decorated with little pictures of a house, animals, birds or flowers.

A sampler had the date, and the name and age of the child who made it.

Design a sampler

Design your sampler on squared paper using coloured crayons or felt-tip pens. Don't make it too complicated. Choose simple patterns for the decoration.

Use different colour embroidery threads and embroidery fabric to make your sampler. Sew simple cross-stitch to create your design.

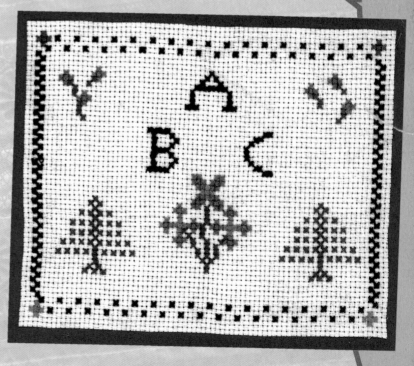

Children at work

Life could be very hard for poor Victorian children. They often worked on farms, down mines and in factories to earn extra pennies to take home. Chimneysweep boys climbed chimneys to clean them. Some **orphans** begged or stole.

Children worked long hours in noisy cotton **mills**.

Life was harsh for young chimneysweeps.

Climbing boys

Victorian houses were heated by coal or wood fires. Boys as young as four were sent up dark, dirty chimneys to clean them. They used a brush and metal scraper to clean off the soot and tar. Sometimes they got stuck or fell into fires.

Older orphans looked after their younger brothers or sisters.

Making changes

Doctor Barnardo was shocked to see children living on the streets in London. He started homes for homeless children.

Lord Shaftesbury was a member of Parliament. He started Ragged Schools for very poor children. Through his work, the use of chimneysweep boys was banned and conditions were improved for children working in factories and down coal mines.

Write a story about a chimneysweep boy

Use the information on these pages to write your story. Draw a picture to illustrate your story.

Joe never wanted to climb another dark, dirty, smelly chimney ever again!

"Hurry up boy!" shouted his master, Mr Pipe

17

Transport

Steam trains and steam ships meant people could travel more easily and cheaply than ever before. Horse-drawn omnibuses and electric trams carried people along busy city streets.

Brunel

Isambard Kingdom Brunel was a famous engineer who built the Great Western Railway between London and Bristol. He wanted his trains to be fast, comfortable and safe.

Brunel built bridges and tunnels which are still used today.

Steam engines

Coal or wood was burned to boil water for the steam that powered the trains. They had to stop regularly for fuel and water.

Queen Victoria made her first train journey on a steam train like this one.

Make a model steam engine

▶ **1** Make the cabin as shown below using a small box and a cardboard tube stuck to the front.

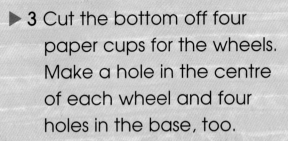

▶ **2** For the base, draw a rectangle on card, the same length and width as the cabin, adding a 3cm border all around.

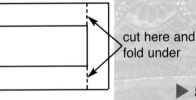

3 cm border — cut here and fold under

Cut along the dotted lines and fold down the border to make a box shape. Stick the base onto the cabin.

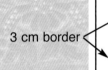

▶ **3** Cut the bottom off four paper cups for the wheels. Make a hole in the centre of each wheel and four holes in the base, too.

▶ **4** Cut two lengths of straw. Push through the holes in the base and attach the wheels. Secure with a piece of Plasticine.

▶ **5** Make a tube of card for the funnel and glue on. Paint the train in bright colours.

Holidays

During the Victorian Age, working days became shorter and wages increased. In 1871, a new law gave them four bank holidays a year. Now they had the time and money for a day trip to seaside resorts such as Blackpool, Brighton and Scarborough.

Foreign travel

Thomas Cook was the first travel firm to arrange foreign tours for wealthier Victorians to Europe, the Holy Land (Israel) and Egypt.

It was fun to go to the beach on bank holidays.

Fun by the sea

Seaside attractions included strolling along the promenade, watching a Punch and Judy show, having a donkey ride or even swimming in the sea!

Posters were colourful and fun.

Design a poster

Design a poster to encourage people to go to the seaside. Include the name of the town and the ticket price. Train tickets cost about 3 **shillings** (s) and 6 pence (d) then, that's 17.5 pence in today's money.

SOUTHERN TRAINS

Brighton

Return ticket only 3s 6d

SKEGNESS

IS SO BRACING

Illustrated Guide from Secretary, Advancement Association, Skegness, or any L·N·E·R Enquiry Office.

What exciting things can you do when you get there?

What picture will you draw?

Victorian towns

Victorian buildings were grand and highly decorated. The building materials were modern – brick, glass, iron and steel. Town halls, schools, shops, stations, museums and churches were built in town centres.

Victorian buildings were built to last so many are still standing and being used today.

The Houses of Parliament are in a famous Victorian building in London.

Part of this city school is Victorian. It has only one floor and very high windows. It is built with red brick an is highly decorated. It looks very different from modern city schools.

Many Victorians schools are still used today.

Find a Victorian building where you live

Learn as much as you can about it. Sketch the building.

▶ **1** First, look at it carefully.

▶ **2** Now draw the shape of the whole building.

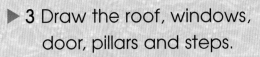

▶ **3** Draw the roof, windows, door, pillars and steps.

▶ **4** Add the decoration.

Famous Victorians

Famous Victorians made Britain a cleaner and healthier place to live.

Florence Nightingale's modern nursing ideas saved many lives. Joseph Lister discovered antiseptic and made operations safer. After the 'Great Stink' caused by sewage waste in 1858, Joseph Bazalgette built London's sewers which are still in use today.

Joseph Bazalgette was a famous Victorian engineer.

Telegraph

Wheatstone and Cooke were engineers who invented a method of sending messages long distances along wires. This was called the telegraph.

Women often worked as telegraph operators.

Morse Code

Telegraphs were sent using a special code called Morse Code invented by Samuel Morse. Morse Code is made up of dots and dashes. It is still used for sending messages today.

A	.-	G	--.	M	--	S	...	Y	-.--	4	....-	Full stop .-.-.-
B	-...	H	....	N	-.	T	-	Z	--..	5	.....	Comma --..--
C	-.-.	I	..	O	---	U	..-	0	-----	6	-....	
D	-..	J	.---	P	.--.	V	...-	1	.----	7	--...	Question ..--..
E	.	K	-.-	Q	--.-	W	.--	2	..---	8	---..	
F	..-.	L	.-..	R	.-.	X	-..-	3	...--	9	----.	

In Morse Code, a dot is a short noise or light flash, a dash is a long noise or flash.

Send a message along a wire

▶ 1 Make a small hole in the bottom of a paper cup.

▶ 2 Thread the string through the cup and a cotton reel.

▶ 3 Cut the ends off two matchsticks and tie one to each end of the string.

▶ 4 Ask a friend to put the paper cup to their ear. Pull the string tight.

▶ 5 You can tap the string or move the matchstick around on the reel to make sounds. Send a message using short and long sounds.

Empire

Victoria was not just Queen of Great Britain, but an Empress of a great empire. By the end of her reign, Queen Victoria ruled over nearly a quarter of the people of the world.

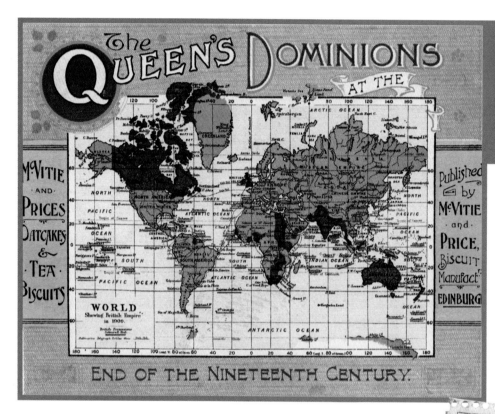

Countries in the Empire were coloured red on the map of the world.

Commonwealth

Today, the Commonwealth is a group of countries that were once part of the Empire.
They support each other and run projects together.

Queen Victoria's head was on stamps of countries in the Empire.

Living abroad

The Empire gave young men exciting job opportunities in the far corners of the world. The children of British families living abroad were often sent home to school and only saw their parents once a year.

A Britsh family living abroad usually had lots of servants.

Trade

The countries of the Empire traded with each other and became richer.

People travelled, learnt new languages and discovered other ways of life.

Dock workers unloading cotton, tea and rubber imported from other countries.

Glossary

Board schools

Free schools for boys and girls which were paid for out of local taxes.

Boarding schools

Schools where children slept and ate during term time.

Empire

A group of countries ruled by an emperor or empress. Queen Victoria was Empress of the British Empire.

Governess

A woman who gives children lessons in their own home.

Household

The people who live together in a single home.

Industry

Work such as coal mining, steel works and making and producing goods in factories.

Middle-class

The group of people who are between the poor and the wealthy. Victorian middle-class men were in business or were doctors and lawyers.

Mill

A factory for making materials, such as cotton or paper.

Nursery

The room in middle- and upper-class homes where children played, slept and had their lessons.

Orphan

Children who have been abandoned or whose parents have both died.

Reign

The period of time a king or queen rules a country.

Sampler

A small piece of embroidery that shows off the skills of the person who has made it.

Shilling

Shillings and pence were the old type of money. There were 12 pence (d) to one shilling (s), and 20 shillings to one pound (£).

Steam engine

An engine in a train or machine which is powered by steam. Steam is the hot gas water becomes when you boil it.

Typhoid

A dangerous disease caught by eating bad food or drinking dirty water. It causes spots, fever and stomach ache.

Working conditions

The state of the places where people work. The working conditions in a Victorian cotton mill were noisy, hot and dusty.

SOUTHERN TRAINS
Brighton

Return ticket only 3s 6d

Index